I
Am South

Donna Snyder
Virgogray Press

VG-48

I Am South © 2010-2014 Donna J. Snyder.

I Am South written by Donna J. Snyder, and published, 2014, by Virgogray Press. All rights reserved by publisher and author. No part of this book may be copied, duplicated, or reproduced, unless in the context of review or analysis, without expressed written permission of the author or publisher.

Second Edition

Cover art by César Iván
Book design by Michael Aaron Casares

ISBN: 978-0692297322
Printed at Createspace
Published by Virgogray Press
Austin, TX, United States of America
http://www.virgograypress.net

I
Am South

Table of Contents

A pastel study in shadows	7
And back story to spare	9
A grackle beautiful and not quite wild	10
Quiet alone	11
In the artist's own words	13
Blame it on Neruda	15
Bliss hangover	16
Thinking of music	17
Brother	18
Cloudy travel by boat	19
Compassion goddess hears the cries of the world	22
Dreaming in cards	23
Dreaming of torture	25
Dreaming in mother of pearl	26
To continue is still imperative	27
Dark red	29
English is an unfortunate language	30
David's best friend	31
Like mocking birds in love	32
The goddess of Willendorf	33
Gushing thunder	34
Jar bottom ashtray	35
Him all Jack Kerouac and shit	36
I am south	37
Like a cloak of many colors	38
I will fear you and lie about it	39
To Octavio Paz who wrote *Concert in the Garden*	40
In the land of women	41
Girl with a whip	43
The perfecter	44
Whisper delicate poet boy	45
The authentic life	46
About the Author	47
Acknowledgments	48

A pastel study in shadow

Part one

Framed pastel
study in shadow
Shady room
Large table
Across from a door
a woman sitting

Light shines clear
through unseen glass
in the room beyond

Hands square in lap
No shoes
A simple shift

Dress the color of a morning glory
minutes after dusk

Part two

Across the table sits
a figure in shadows
Person or perhaps spirit

Or perhaps the dark side
she aims to conquer
through direct scrutiny

Light reflected from
the table's surface
does not illuminate the shadow

This seems to be about loss
Caught up in shades of mourning
All grays and blacks and purples

Part three

She sits alone with her guest
in the non-light of dusk
Her feet firm on the floor

Calls it by name without distress
Hands warm on sloped thighs

When the light fades
the shade will eat
the lilac dust

And back story to spare

You dominate the moving picture of my life now
Today you are foreground
Monday as I rush through a world of sorrow
you will be background
Each day we grow into each other
entwined like roses in a mountain ballad
It frames the picture of my life and sends its roots
deep into your subconscious
You stroke skin and it dances through the sky
You light my way to emptied-ness
Take me somewhere new
Forgotten waters boil and continents shift
Paint my flesh
Brocade desire across my back
Loosen my grasp on now or then
Know me even though you do not know me
Take me into a blue cave
Crawl inside my way of being and make it your home
Draw your madness on my feet with henna
Gold leaf my beauty across your consciousness
Seize this moment
Find the important thing
It waits for you within the secrets of a lived life
Brave the deep waters
Dive into my deepest truth
Find me waiting
Find me
You know you will
You know you have

A grackle beautiful and not quite wild

Those eyes
Now green
Now blue
From time to time gray
Mutable as your personae

A grackle beautiful and not quite wild
Quick to spy odd treasure and seize it
You become succulent in a hostile land

In love you laugh anger out loud
Lash at the ever present dangers
Brave foreignness and the crazy streets
You claim the affections of all you meet

You the jesting savior of the untouched heart

And so damned pretty

Quite alone

As if the world is weeping

Pacific waves break hard and my feet lift off
submerged completely those long seconds
I scream fear and heartache into the tide's assault
When it recedes I stand and walk against the waves
My eyes on the sunset's corona I walk toward Japan
Each time the waves engulf me I scream like murder
I scream endless screams then stand up in the ebb
I walk toward Japan until limp from ongoing struggle
emptied just for this moment of fear and heartache
But I know I won't get to Japan walking into the sea
so I remove my emptied self out of the mother's belly
Back to some unknown shore and its desert bed

As if the world would weep for me

As if the world weeps the way I do
Great sheets of rain against a window
Great gasps of air rattle the rafters
The door slams shut and the shingles pop
I close my eyes and hide my eyes beneath
the soiled comfort of cotton and feathers
My belly begins to unfold the fist inside it
After a time I am able to soothe myself
I begin to hear as the storm subsides

When the wind dies

The relentless rains begin to quell as well
When the gales become quiet the neighbor
can be heard pitiful as an abandoned child

As if the world really were weeping also
the way she does when the violence is past
The slamming door hangs silent half ajar
A woman swallows her sobs to an artificial silence
Behind her chest bone they collect and coagulate

Her sorry nose drips like the last sorry raindrops
still falling from the roof top onto the stone path
Closing the window she wipes away the wild water
She finds herself quite pacific and quiet alone

In the artist's own words

2000 frames in 3 minutes
art as labor intensive exposition of non-narrative beliefs
random images fall from whatever is at hand
the chaos stirred by the wing of an insect
a coupon from Walgreens for catsup or mustard
the seduction of money & the lowest impulses
the artist picks up this object and drops it onto that canvas
like a gift to a lover who won't accept who you are
hidden among the autum leaves like an old photograph
a beautiful girl with brown eyes
like jewels on a royal cape of feathers

the lascivious tongue
the nose rimmed in white
the slobber & mumbles of subterfuge
the bread of life
the body of Christ
a man or a woman with sorrowful eyes
a woman in shades of plum wanting to suck out your life
then disappear into the night
one more time

the artist is looking for someone to trust
but the only place to find that person is on the other
side of the mirror
the body is broken & bloody
entrails spell out your name in the end
the question is can something be made from nothing
2000 frames in 3 minutes

Nietsche said that's what makes artsts special
something from nothing so the rules don't apply
Neitsche killed himself in a madhouse
out of the mouth of madness--

out of the poisons we take into our body--
we find truth

bloodsoaked cloth tied around our wrists painting
the beginning of the story

someone else's story
his story
my story

a contrived chaos
a fallen & broken wing

Blame it on Neruda

If only I had never said yes to Pablo Neruda
how different my life would be now
But, no, I said yes yes yes and yes

the compelling eroticism
the insistent imagery
the smells of earth and flesh

the sound of movies and silk hosiery swishing
the young thighs crossed and uncrossed in the darkness
If only I had never said yes to fervent kisses beneath my ear

If only I had retired alone to my concrete
bed and orange cobija
used the Neruda for a pillow
slept with my legs in a tight knot
But no, I could not say no and Neruda had his way with me

If only I had not acted out the Conquest with you
Me Malinche and you the white rapacious hordes
No
You already knew I read Neruda in the humid night

And with that you knew everything you needed to know
Desire conflated with need and any action thereby justified
I said hello to the conquest of the Americas in reverse

If only I had ignored the sound of fuschia flowers blooming
in the night
I blame it all on Neruda
And now I'm poetry's slave

Bliss hangover

she fell down his stairs
he celebrated with tequila
he knew what he wanted
she did not
incapable of escaping a bliss hangover
just another fallen angel on the border
without any extra strength lotion
to calm the desertscape of her skin

Thinking in music

In the midnight hours dark and lonely as an unmarked grave, rage and weeping make a cadence. Audible despair rises and falls. It beats like wings ceaseless before the gusts and torrents of an unpredicted storm.

"I can't write," I think. "The music is where I come from," I think. "Bread and water, the glory of light, a cracked and open heart."

Images flee. Here there is no Word. Here there is no language. Seeing no deliverance, rage and weeping echoes in the dark.

I am waiting for the light of revelation. From the distance a murmur grows loud.

I do not see him.

Brother

Take my hand
Brother
We can lie
together
on the white line
holding hands
We can dance
thru tinsel stars
Forget the damage
of baby days
Laugh at being
strange
The blue cross
beckons
Take my hand
Brother
We can dance
away the rage
We can dance
away the pain
We can dance
away the shame
I have missed you
long years Brother
Take my hand
We can dance

Cloudy travel by boat

> *Be patient with everything*
> *unresolved in your heart and try*
> *to love the questions themselves*
> *as if they were locked rooms or*
> *books written in a very*
> *unfamiliar language.*
> —Rilke

I woke up just a nasty specter in someone else's anxiety nightmare.
Animated computer graphics and acid dream gave me a headache.
Trapped in Linklater's ponderings on the meaning of life.
Captured to be rewound and reviewed as much as desired.
From one brainy chat to another I wander and wonder
who is the star among these vigorous emanations from real lives,
worrying about the positive implications of existentialism,
quantum physics, post modernism, beauty and truth and such.

I feel transient now for no one knows me
where I work or live.
Perhaps I am just asleep in a waiting room that smells of farts,
or maybe drowsing through my stop on a subway through existence.
There was a train trip but then there was some cloudy travel by boat.
Like Iris Murdoch, I fell down a stairway
and wound up with a life mate.
She said she always wrote about the search for honesty and beauty.
I breathe into my momentary existence to loose myself

from those limits.
Lost in someone else's lucid dream I cannot find my way
back to power.

Someone remembers a monologue from a demented person.
She shuffled from gray room to another room that's yellow,
mumbling and shouting fervent prayers for one in pink,
forgetting that no one listened to her when she sang or
wept.
The thing about her work, they say, was the use of visuals.

She always claimed it was a political act just to give voice,
but the only thing anyone ever remembered was the sex.
The act of observing her turned her into something else.

I rarely feel the courage to peer into a dusty mirror's
dim glass,
the dead wander in and out the mirror's frame
of reference.
I flounder lost among random reveries of unspecified dead.
There is an electric heart sharp red
against the bruised autumn sky.
An electric cloud hulas around the scarlet shape
like a nimbus.
The weather warns me that shadows approach always
and soon.

I wonder if someone will stand beside me,
clutch the bone hand.
Calaveras prance across the mantel where I live
but they are mute.
I do not feel at home here now that my mind has no weight,
me nothing but contingent the way Beauvoir used the word.
I am squatting in a house that could be mine
but I don't know.

Calaveras dance for those gone and for those still to come.

I sit in growing dark and hope someone left signs
to help me find the road.

Compassion goddess hears the cries of the world

I came here on the back of an extinct crane,
riding its slender neck,
wings fierce and gilded with the feathers of the north wind.
I heard the needs of the people and the tormented world.
I fled the other place and came to the border
of here and there.
Don't measure my strength by the standards
of your own desires.
Do not judge my beauty by the light of the eyes you behold
in the obsidian mirror.
Plumb my darkness and encounter your own illumination.
Herald my compassion and celebrate the outrage
in my heart.
Look me in the face and dare to see me,
now sorrowful,
now ashiver with ecstasy.
You may be blinded by the stars about my head.
Twist my hair into a knot and bind me to your fate.
You may be blinded
but I will not look away.
There is no existence without the "I."
There is no authenticity without the "now."

Dreaming in cards

I.

The crown is reversed
Aristocrat becomes exile
He turns his feathered back on the siren's song
A choice will lead him back to the horned man's woodland
I have had enough he says
but she has permeated the matter with her strangeness
A girl rows her lover into the past
Her lap is filled with paper flowers
She becomes a broken crown and rolls
through an open door
Poets drunk on brandied words weave
the record of love and battle
A knave turns a lady on her head in the middle
of the royal highway
In the dream of the querent
many cups shine like silvered stars

II.

I have a habit of finding men who believe in fate
The way the rains fell like a god's seed falls on earth
Or maybe destiny foretold in a tumble down a narrow stairs
His mark left on me here and here and mine left there
In that first meeting I become entangled in his desire
My body responds like tango from a box switched to on
The desire may dim but the passion is a stain
like words on a page
Like the smell of flowers whose flesh is bruised and torn

III.

In the evening the voice of Death caresses dusty air

in a dim room
Tropical music stirs me to move my flesh
in time to guitar and drum

I recall I once kept poetry in a rainbow
on my speckled wrist
Yet that was a time when the future
was never seen as kind

IV.

Rains fall like a god's seed on the earth
Seeds fall like words on a page

Dreaming of torture

You stand over me
my prince of self-destruction
Immolation brings an emptiness that is almost peace
I lay prostrate at your little feet
my bottom big and inviting your touch
I am confident of you
swallow you whole
take you in
permit you to see me this way
you see me looking never knowing
You stand there groaning as I become music
I sing
I am a wordless song
I scream music
I know love if at all here at your feet
falling into that sublime oblivion
You feel power over me
You dream of victims
Your beauty dies
My beauty flees
I am no goddess
You are no god
There is no god
There is no music
There is no beauty
only victims
and you see me
prostrate at your feet

Dreaming in mother of pearl

Small breasts and fat rolls
Body of an immortal beauty
The Goddess of love and righteous indignation
Aphrodite
She rose fleshy and pristine from the foam of the infinite sea
Unlike her sister Athena
who sprang from the imperfect brow of the father god
Aphrodite is unmeasured and without flaw
Small breasts and fat rolls
The image transcends the span of centuries
I feel the abundant flesh against my face
Small breasts and fat rolls
Blood and breath dance through my mortal body
I close my eyes and dream in mother of pearl

To continue is still imperative

my dreams have been strange lately
I know this although I do not remember them
but the recollection of a recent dream appears in my mind
from time to time
it is a black night and I dive over and over
from the prow of a black boat
into the blackest water
the moment of the dive repeats itself
like a scratched phonograph record
no sense of water or air on my skin
no wet slickness
my lungs do not strain for air
my body neither heaves itself out of the water
nor onto the boat
I see the water and I dive, then see dark water again
and then dive again
I have no idea where I am nor why I would dive
into the inky deep
I don't know if it is ocean, river, harbor or lake
all I know is I am alone and the world is black
and while there is no urgency
to continue is still imperative
I do not touch the bottom
I do not find treasure or hidden horrors,
just an endless prison of flesh impelled
to move through the dark with no end in sight
and no thought in mind,
devoid of content
when I wake up I wonder where in my life I am reawakening
I listen to the blood in my ears until I recall who I am now
it's like that in the dream
no one to gather me in their eyes and wrap me
in robes of daylight and color
just the darkest night
the blackest depths

in the distance I hear music
released from its round black prison one last time
before all its kind are broken
I close my eyes and write down the words
but I forget to sing along

Dark red

Dark red I love Lucy lips make me long
for cigarettes and sex

She stands in the shadows like a Botticelli made of marzipan
Who wouldn't want to slip sweet almond beneath the
tongue?
Lips linger and intoxicate themselves beneath the pearl of
an ear
Inhale the scent of flesh still warm from an indifferent sun
still moist from the exertion of making sense of the lives of
men
all gone mad with sorrow

We sit and laugh at the antics of a crazy redhead goddess
The voice of an angel sings
We must not forget to breathe

Deep humid gulps of warm air swallowed
like wine drunk from a terracotta cup
a red kiss pressed against its earthy lip

English is an unfortunate language

abstractions are both easy and hard
easy to gush or fall into the larded syrup of cliche
difficult to capture the original detail of the scent of sky
the shade of the juice that stains your fingers and lips
again I am suspended over the abyss of words and meaning

alone in the bath I let the water become tepid
unbidden the words and music form themselves
in my mouth
blue fills the room like cool steam
images rhythms tones hang in the air
no one hears but me and not even I remember
the words or tune
as the dirtied water swirls and leaves me chilled and wet
and listening to something like silence

David's best friend

five shots of tequila later
she wonders to herself
about David's best friend
before he left for the war
bound to break her heart
determined to fight for freedom

she suffers the hang-over alone
with she herself and I imagine
fair weather friends all of 'em
happy ever after is real she scoffs
as the efficacy of revolution
the ethereality of passion

when her brain ceases its hot throbbing
she looks at the vomit next to her feet
if she were a dog she would eat each bit
nothing would remain to even desiccate
in the furnace she calls the desert wind
in the stony world she calls her home
nothing is left here
not even his scent

Like mockingbirds in love

dreams have winding meaning
        in and out of focus
roads going over the embittered
        loss, anxiety, flight & silence
earth, labyrinthine paths
        clamber through the night sky

parks in flower, in darkness and in silence
        like nightingales in love with the moon
deep vaults, ladders over the stars
        yet lost in sorrow
altar pieces of hopes and memories
        blue glass shines again in windows

tiny men walk past and smiling
        they're not his but the artist
likes having them around
        melancholy toys of old people--
a headless Buddha, forgotten fans
        photographs and sweet visions

a mockingbird sings
        at the flowering turn in the road
a pomegranate promises sweetness and seeds
        to no one
and mythical monsters, rosy ones
        a fallen angel newly chaste

that wanders far away
        dances alone
sits in the dark
        moans sweet and low

The goddess of Willendorf

breasts sagged and without symmetry
many pendulous bellies attest to use
the braided face of the mysteries
an erotic fetish
small enough to fit in your palm
always available to fondle and caress
carried by the faithful on a thong about the neck
buried with fervent prayers for abundance and fecundity
beneath a pine bough bed

Gushing thunder

the rasp of a voice making rain
tonguing the catgut of the throat

strange laughter engulfs the mitochondria

the electro-convulsive shock therapy of sin

a fluid fever
envelops
with
the
odor
of
your
hair

Jar bottom ashtray

It's just another blues song written at a kitchen table
Jar bottom ashtray sweating butts
Mass confusion
Decipherless jumbles
Sweet submission sublimely devoid of pain
The ceaseless rhythm
I hear children calling where there are no children playing
There are no children crying here
No children here
The feminine pronoun
how intimate it becomes so fast
And it becomes so quickly self-revelatory
Nonetheless I regret each letter that remains unwritten
Savages are saints who need to lie in grasses
for hours on end
free of broom
I become lost in idle wanderings through mazes
obstructed episodically by bowlers and canes
Monstrous images hastening a curtain's graceless flight
across the plains of aging sight
Hold the fine print closer to the crumbling eye
Sexual perversity it says
Its pitfalls and pranks
I want something here
Some fortuitous reprise of a motif
Boundaries
Borders
The management of process

Him all Jack Kerouac and shit

him all Jack Keroac and shit
his biography an artist's cliche
oh he told a good anecdote yes
took her to his garrett to see the view
she let him dry her with skin and lips
all happy in the moment he kissed her hair

her all this is only just for now you know
an ephemeral spring so drink up fast
when it ended she hardly noticed
lost so was she in grief for pretty words
mirror shards piled like minnowy regrets
all caught up in the moment she almost knew

I am south

There were once women who made many kings
by taking a mate
The tacit memory of them inhabits me
like stones left to mark my way
The blood of Northern tribes undeniably runs
through my body
My hair is reddish and my skin pale
with cinnamon flecks
but I am South
Gravity pulled me from north to south
to find some truer self
South is where I learned to swallow Pablo Neruda
like rum
South is where time stretches out like a bus trip
in exotic lands
And south is where I can both swear and sweat
in Spanish
There is antiquity here everywhere
and I have become part of it
The inscrutable past etched across desertscapes
like ghost buttes
The scattered and desiccated detritus of other lives lived
and other loves
Effulgent planes and circles circling out
through time and space
like ephemeral water

The humid kiss of desert stones
I am south

Like a cloak of many colors

I can't write subtleties by nature
I articulate experience in blatant terms
I name the emotion
Wear it like a cloak of many colors
to demonstrate how I am one of the chosen
I wallow in graphic descriptions of acts born in feelings
Shove my nose into the dark folds of existence and scream
your name
I cannot write in ambiguities
My job is to name a thing and make its existence
compel response
I live loud
Bring your secrets to me and I will write them big
across an empty wall
Plant them in a city garden
Erect a sign describing them to the idle passers by
You know what I mean by the way I say it
I throw my weight around and underscore my meaning
with urgence
Passion does not vitiate my rationality
I can feel and think at the same time
I trumpet and drum your beauties
I call attention to defects and dance their name
to the rhythm of the streets
I crawl beneath your skin and make it home
"In ugliness beauty may be found but in prettiness never"
I forge a truth from shadows and make it mine

I will fear you and lie about it

Stay here with me
your life a forfeit for my desire
Feed me and tell me what I need to hear

But I won't listen
I'll kiss your presence only
when I'm gone cold and lonely
In the dark streets of my anger
I will fear you and lie about it

I can't reach out
I lock the door and douse the light
Lying silent in the darkness until I trip

Then I pounce
anger in my eyes like a spiked helmet
I rub excreta in your face with an unlovely touch
My ferocious aspect

The ugliness of sorrow justifies your torment
The absence of my compassion rips out my own heart

To Octavio Paz who wrote *Concert in the Garden*

It rains.
The hour is an enormous eye.
Inside it we come and go like reflections.
The river of music enters my blood.
If I say body, it answers wind.
If I say body, it answers when.
If I say earth, it answers where.
The world, a double blossom, opens.
Sadness of having come.
Joy of being here.
I walk lost in my own scents.

In the land of women

Silver branches drench the air with enchantments
A flock of night birds sings the beloved to sleep
He dreams of mama and his mouth aches to suck
but nothing compares to her breast
So he sucks his fist and goes to bed hungry
In sleep he rubs himself and knows he is a man

Years pass waiting for the end of silence
wandering sad through restless dreams
wishing for comrades and a bit of home
Silver wands grow bent and brittle
"The magic is gone," women say to one another
Tree limbs whisper wearily of lost loves

Beneath the singing tree a spring calls
hidden as the limpid eye of god
Times past mountain women gathered
to eat sweetmeats
Voices raised in song and laughter
Tall tales told of love and terror

Women dancing drunk on clear spring water
pure and phosphorescent as god's eye is cold
The spring was fresh as honest words
Now the death dry trees are quiet and still
Stream stagnant below a shroud of rotted leaves
Water fouled with the feces of dying birds

The beloved cries for the end of silence
He wanders addled and sad in search of no one
Now all are lost in the lonely desert
The wind turns their flesh to cholla and stone
Nights are hot and heedless beneath unloving stars

The beloved wanders aimlessly through the thorns

Wishes for night birds to sing him back to sleep
Wishes for mama's sugared breast and lips

Girl with a whip

A child with a whip
Solemn eyes the color of coffee
Limp wrist hangs down
The whip almost forgotten drags the dirt
Her patient shoes tied with black ribbon
Grosgrain ribbon
The kind that makes good bows
Lips not yet ready to be kissed
Those brown eyes stare directly into thoughts
that even you did not know you knew
That even you never knew in your most lucid dream

The perfecter

A genderless soul
    Spiraling signs of the triple goddess omnipresent
The four paths,
Petals of truth marking the way
    Inside an effulgent spirit meditating on how and when
A caldron
A sword
A spear
A stone pillar
The universe dreaming of you
    Aspiration more than prescriptive
The ultimate outcome
The final destination
    Integration more than perfection
The effulgent universe held within

Whisper delicate poet boy

Caramel breast let me lick
our secret death
Whisper delicate poet boy
Unravel my naked soul
Dance ferocious magic
over my skin
Eyes dazzled
Warm current
Blue perfume
Essential universe

The Authentic Life

in this heat the man sweats
he hammers pain and anger
flakes and strips away the past
ancient errors melt
the real thing naked
well-worn but genuine
open and spontaneous
unmasked and letting go
laughter packs rage and pain in boxes
moves them out
sees the detritus of lives lived fleeing
it burns the past like unpaid bills
a magnificent largeness swells
life waltzes through blue glass caves
see it shimmer

About the author

Donna Snyder's *Poemas ante el Catafalco: Grief and Renewal* was published by Chimbarazu Press in 2014. In 2015, NeoPoiesis Press will release her poetry collection, *Three Sides of the Same Moon*. She is working on a poetry collection for Slough Press.

Snyder also publishes work in literary journals and anthologies throughout the United States and on-line, and has presented readings in Sitka, Alaska, Boston, New York City, Denver, Southern California and throughout New Mexico and Texas. She is a contributing poetry editor to *Return to Mago* and her book reviews appear in *Red Fez*, the *El Paso Times,* and other venues.

Snyder's work as an activist lawyer advocating on behalf of indigenous people, immigrant workers, and people with disabilities has garnered multiple prizes and recognitions. She founded the Tumblewords Project in 1995, and continues to coordinate its free weekly workshops and other events.

Acknowledgements of publication

The following poems or variations of them have appeared or will appear in other publications, to the editors of which grateful acknowledgement is made.

"Compassion goddess hears the cries of the world," *Return to Mago* and *Three Sides of the Same Moon*

"Dreaming in mother of pearl," *Return to Mago* and *Three Sides of the Same Moon*

"The goddess of Willendorf," *Return to Mago* and *Three Sides of the Same Moon*

"Gushing thunder," *Unlikely Stories 2.0*

"In the land of women," *Three Sides of the Same Moon*

"The perfecter," *Three Sides of the Same Moon*

"Whisper delicate poet boy," *Poemas ante el Catafalco: Grief and Renewal*

More Poetry Titles Available from Virgogray Press

NO FEAR by Doctori Sadisco
In the Broken Things by Gillian Prew
Vegas Implosions by Chris D'Errico
By the Banks of the Ajoy, Jaideb Vanishes into the Blue by Subhankar Das
Elektra's Mouth by Suzi Kaplan Olmsted
Elephants I Didn't Ride by Peter Marti
You Are Not a Normal Human Being by Justin Blackburn
Sinister Splashplay by David S. Pointer
Ministry of Kybosh by Chris D'Errico
The End of Mythology by A. Molotkov & John S. Williams
Carcinogenic Poetry Anthology Volume 1-2
Nothing. No One. Nowhere. # 2-5
Beneath Our Feet by Mary B. Harrison

www.virgograypress.net

www.ingramcontent.com/pod-product-compliance
Lightning Source LLC
LaVergne TN
LVHW051807080426
835511LV00019B/3431